> You created the life you have.
> What do you need
> to create to have the life
> you want?
>
> *Shani Richards*

Copyright © 2022 by Books Here Books There

All rights reserved. No part of this book may be reproduced or used in any manner without written permission of the copyright owner except for the use of quotations in a book review. For more information:
info@booksherebooksthere.com

ISBN 978-1-7367874-6-5 (print)
ISBN 978-1-7367874-7-2 (digital)

Publishing to Books Here Books There

www.visionpartnerjournal.com

Printed in the USA

The Vision Partner Journal

The Vision Partner Journal

Your Invitation

To Declare	To Inspire	To Recognize
Love	**Hope**	**Purpose**

Shani Richards | Tina Robinson | Larrisa Stevens-Poree

Books Here Books There Publishing LLC
2022 - New York, New York

This Journal
Belongs to

....

The Vision Partner Journal

Your Inspiration *Topics*

The messages and reflections in this journal are yours to explore in whichever order meets the needs of your season, day, or moment. Go in page order or out of page order. Use a reflection for a day, or for a deeper dive, remain with a reflection for a week or longer.

The column alongside each reflection invites you to date and/or note each entry. Periodically go back to written entries and read what you have expressed. Notice what has changed, what has developed, what has been revealed, what has been resolved or removed.

Our Collaboration	08
Get To know Us	09
Dedication	10
Welcome	11
Declare Love	12
I Am Loveable	14
I Am Creating	15
I Am Easy To Love	16
I Am A Voice	17
I Transcend All	18
I Make Choices	19
Love Is My Divine Birthright	20
Freedom Resides Within Me	21
I Respond To Love	22
I Bathe In Self-Approval	23

The Vision Partner Journal

Inspire Hope — 24

Don't Let What Others Have Done Stop You	26
Always Leave Them Better	27
With All The Hats, Wear Your Hat of Hope	28
If You Want, Give	29
Today Is Yours	30
Life Is Taking Care Of One Another	31
Lift Others	32
We Need Windows Of Opportunity	33
We Will Be Fine	34
Keep Looking Higher	35
Expect Great Things	36
The Chapter Of Your Life	37

Recognize Purpose — 38

Your Success Isn't Out Of Reach	40
See What You Want Before It Manifests	41
There's Room At The Top	42
Live By Intention	43
Create The Life You'd Risk It All To Have	44
Life's Seasons Change	45
Finishing Creates Confidence	46
Reignite Your Passion	47
Your Thoughts Are Your Truth	48
You Are Practicing You	49

Blank Pages — 50

Our Collaboration *Journey*

I would like to introduce Tina Robinson, Optimist Coach, and Larrisa Stevens Poree, New Thought Spiritual Practitioner. Both served as amazing thought partners during my own journey and have joined me as co-authors of this Journal. I am excited to share our vision and words as we support you to see and achieve your vision.

I knew these ladies independently and when I was in a season of stretching my belief, I did something intentional. I reached out to them specifically to ask if they would be my vision partners as I sought to develop and launch a retreat. I needed them for the retreat and I needed them for me. I was full of hope and knew that I had gotten as far as I could on my own. I knew from my past experiences and patterns that soon I would stop. Not because I was tired but because my vision was bigger than I could carry out alone.

My time with Larrisa and Tina reminds me of when I had failed to run a mile in 7th grade. To pass means I had to run it in 10 minutes or less and this was my last chance. I was always winded and could faintly taste blood with my inhale and exhales. A girl named Neffy and her best friend finished their mile and came back on the route to get me. They started off with encouraging words and then they got on either side of me and ran, pulled, and told me I could make it. I did make it and I know I would not have passed if it wasn't for them.

Larrisa and Tina were necessary in case I got winded or even distracted. Having them as part of the planning and their commitment to being with me on the journey was fuel to me. It ended up being just us three and we received that with an understanding that if it was only us 3, it was what it needed to be. We went through the entire retreat following the program that we had designed to take others through and we took ourselves through it.

We stayed up late talking and the insights that we shared with one another were revealing and personal. I remember receiving so much – why did I feel the need to do so much without inviting others to help? Wouldn't I be an imposition if I asked for help in areas that I was capable of doing or incapable of doing on my own? Wow, there wasn't a whole lot of room in my thinking for me to ask for help or invite others in. How could I delegate what I was capable of doing? If I wanted to inspire independence in others, why was I so committed to doing so much on their behalf or inconvenience myself but strive to think of every conceivable way that I could make their path easier? Incongruence. I was so blessed to receive the loving and honest observation and input.

We came back from the Retreat with a great deal of confirmation that our paths were intersecting for a purpose and the inspiration to see what that could look like.

This journal is an expression of what we have crafted from that time together and our separate work and areas of focus. We have intentionally crafted through words a powerful series of inspiration, questions, and reflections to reveal or clarify the voices within the most powerful people we know – All of Us, and that includes You.

Get to Know us

Shani
Author, Publisher, and Speaker

She is a natural introvert and practiced extrovert who loves to serve and equip women to live a life filled with purpose. She is known for delivering positive and inspirational messages that address purpose and destiny. She has a knack for creatively and strategically supporting others to identify what it takes for them to move beyond their "good intentions" into action and completion.

You can stay in contact with Shani online at **www.shanirichards.com**, and **www.booksherebooksthere.com** and Instagram **@BooksHereBooksThere**, and ClubHouse **@ShaniRichards**

Larrisa
President & CEO of Courageous Life Insurance Group

Larrisa is the President & CEO of Courageous Life Insurance Group in which she specializes in helping her clients secure end of life plans that give honor to their legacy while also honoring the ones left behind. As a speaker and trainer, Larrisa's message delivers what she knows to be an undeniable truth, which is that she is whole, perfect, and complete, and so are you!

You can stay in contact with Larrisa on Instagram **@UniversalLoveJunkie**; FaceBook **Larrisa Stevens-Poree**; and ClubHouse **@Larrisaporee**

Tina
President and Founder of Optimistic Coach

Known as a natural optimist, she can find a positive perspective out of just about every situation. Tina is committed to community and has a vested interest in the next generation.

She is the co-founder of Pathway to Excellence, a coaching program for teens. Pathway to Excellence has a focus on academic excellence and the development of strong life skills. As a minister, she has a passion for servant leadership and for training and empowering others to seek their purpose and true potential. Her sweet spot is helping others discover theirs. Tina is a true cheerleader of people and their passions and serves as a confidant and a safe place of accountability.

You can stay in contact with Tina **CoachT@BooksHereBooksThere.com**

Dedication

This book is dedicated to *you*.

Dedicated to your mind, body, spirit, and spice

Dedicated to what you think makes you *naughty* and *nice*

Dedicated to you when you are dedicated and true

Dedicated to you when you lose track of you

Dedicated to you when you travel comfortably and light

Dedicated to you when you're burdened and can't keep up the fight

To you when your *heart is full* and bursting at the seams

To you when you feel broken, sour, and mean

To you at every twist and turn of your brilliant life's show

Because no matter what or who, you are committed to grow

Grow with the confidence that you are worth the effort and will benefit from every life lesson. We have imagined you succeeding and are rooting for you every step of the way.

You matter

Welcome to Your Journal

In this journal, we are sharing our three distinct voices to support your exploration, reflection, and inspiration as you journey to the YOU that you know, dream, and have imagined that you ARE. Yes, the magnificent person that you already are is in you, leaving clues, speaking urgently at times and at times softly.

You are not alone on this journey or in the journal. We are your Vision Partners and the inspiration in these pages is provided to help you in whichever order you decide meets the needs of your season, day, or moment. Go in or out of page order. Explore a page for a day, week, or even a month. Here are some examples of how you can navigate through the pages.

Possible Paths

Chronological Path
You crave order because it fuels your sense of security and appreciation for certainty. You prefer a straightforward approach for creating a routine so **Go in section and page order**

Curated Path
You enjoy having some input in what you do and when you do it so **Choose your section order**, for example (1) Hope (2) Love (3) Purpose **and go in page order through each section OR select the topic that you need each day, week, or month**

Hybrid Path
You have a routine and tools that you enjoy AND you like a little variation from time to time. Why choose? **Periodically** you can **include this journal in your existing practice**, you get to set how often and which topics.

The column alongside each page invites you to date your entries. Periodically go back to written entries and read what you have expressed. Notice what has changed, what has developed, what has been revealed, what has been resolved or removed.

You are *magnificent* be *curious, studious* and *compassionate* about you.

Page 11

Declare Love

Larrisa Poree
Universal Love Junkie

Oh my goodness! I am so excited that you are here. I am a solid believer that life is not only our master teacher but it will also meet us at our level of courage!

As you read and journey through these next few pages, I want to remind you that life is inviting you to be courageous enough to do the work of slowing down, extending grace to yourself, and fully frolic in the beauty of the prompts presented to you within these pages. Have fun with them, be silly, cry, laugh and be courageous enough to be amazed by who you are so that you may declare absolute Love for yourself. Do all of this simply because you deserve it.

I am loveable

Declaration
Today, I will whisper to myself that "I am Loveable" and by the end of the day, that whisper will become a resounding vibration that permeates every cell in my body.

Reflection
Time to scan your body. Lie down and repeat this affirmation and imagine your words breathing life into the many parts of your body.

Sequence
- From the toes of both feet to the tops and soles of your feet, and then on to your ankles
- Calves
- Knees
- Thighs
- Pelvic region- includes hips & genitals. Next, move to your Stomach and waist, then your
- Lower back (tailbone & buttocks)
- Chest, upper back- shoulder & shoulder blades, hands (wrists, fingers, fingernails, palms, top of hand)
- Arms (forearm, upper arm, elbows)
- Neck, face and head (jaw, lips, nose, chin, cheeks, ears, eyes, forehead, scalp, top of your head)

Declaration

Right now, I detach myself from speaking, thinking, or acting like a victim. Instead, I joyfully embrace the good that I am creating in my life right now.

Reflection

Pick a superhero (preferably one that wears a cape) see yourself as that superhero. Imagine yourself rescuing yourself from the unruly thoughts that you may use to put yourself down. Replace those thoughts with words and images of self-empowerment.

....	....
....	....
....	....
....	....
....	....
....	....
....	....
....	....
....	....
....	....
....	....
....	....
....	....
....	....
....	....
....	....
....	....
....	....
....	....
....	....
....	....
....	....

Declaration

Right now, I detach myself from speaking, thinking, or acting like a victim. Instead, I joyfully embrace the good that I am creating in my life right now.

Reflection

Pick a superhero (preferably one that wears a cape) see yourself as that superhero. Imagine yourself rescuing yourself from the unruly thoughts that you may use to put yourself down. Replace those thoughts with words and images of self-empowerment.

.... | ....
.... | ....
.... | ....
.... | ....
.... | ....
.... | ....
.... | ....
.... | ....
.... | ....
.... | ....
.... | ....
.... | ....
.... | ....
.... | ....
.... | ....
.... | ....
.... | ....
.... | ....
.... | ....
.... | ....

I am a voice

Declaration
I Am a voice for myself and I use it liberally.

Reflection
Use your smart phone or recording device to record yourself saying powerful, empowering, and encouraging I Am statements (I Am kind, I Am a masterful communicator, I Am free to be ME, etc.). Listen to the recording while you navigate (in the car, while cooking, etc.) throughout your day.

I transcend all

Declaration
I am peace and I transcend all manner of stress.

Reflection
Recite this affirmation 3 times silently with your eyes open.
Next, silently recite the affirmation again with your eyes closed and one hand on your heart.
Lastly, recite the affirmation, but this time light a candle (physically or in your mind) and as the smoke rises from the candle, imagine yourself transcending all of your worries while being deeply rooted in peace, which is represented by the candle.

I make choices

Declaration
I make incredible choices that benefit me and the people in my realm of influence.

Reflection
Imagine your choices being the life-giving energy that lights the world, that turns frowns into smiles, and brings nourishment to famished places. Now move throughout your day with this measure of self-esteem.

Love is my divine birthright

Declaration
Love, laughter, healing, and prosperity are my divine birthright.

Reflection
Spend the next five minutes picturing yourself extending and receiving Love, laughter, healing, and prosperity in the same way in which you breathe: EFFORTLESSLY!!!

Freedom resides within me

Declaration
In this very moment, I affirm that the key to my freedom resides within me.

Reflection
Write out this affirmation 10 times and keep it in a place in which you can easily make reference to it throughout the day. Commit to allowing yourself to really feel free!

I respond to love

Declaration
I no longer respond to manipulation, drama, or suffering. Instead, I respond to Love, compassion, grace, and joy!

Reflection
Look at yourself in the mirror and repeat this affirmation 10 times at least 3 times a day (morning, afternoon, and night).

I bathe in self-approval

Declaration
I bathe myself in self-approval.

Reflection
Look in the mirror and silently recite the affirmation 5 times. Now recite the affirmation 5 times out loud (as loud as you feel able to do so). Lastly, take a shower and as the water is running over your perfect and glorious body, recite the affirmation 10 times. As you are reciting the affirmation in the shower, imagine yourself speaking life into the areas of your life in which you require your own sweet blessings.

Inspire Hope

Tina Robinson
Optimistic Coach

I'm told that I only see the good in things, at times, naive. This is the thing, is it easier to see something for you or against you? Life is a series of ebbs and flows, sometimes we're up, and sometimes we're down.

At times it's due to our own doing or at the hands of another. Trusting in the hope that it does not disappoint, whatever Life brings, we will be okay. Hard times make us stronger; uncertainty lends itself to possibility; momentary trials lead to our triumph. It is written, hope deferred makes a heart sick, but a desire fulfilled is a Tree of Life. Hope is the Tree of Life that continues to stand up in us despite the storms. Never apologize for expecting something good to come into your situation, even situations that appear hopeless. As you read these simple thought-provoking prompts, may the strength of your character awaken the hope in you to endure another day!

Don't let what others have done stop you

Inspiration
At last count, 7.5 billion people in the world, but one you. Don't let what others have done stop you from doing you.

Reflection
Now what?

Inspiration

When it comes to people, places and things, always leave them better than you found them.

Reflection

For the next seven days, commit to leaving things better than you found them.
(Record your acts)

With all the hats, wear your hat of hope

Inspiration
With all the hats we will wear in our lifetime, never go without your hat of hope.

Reflection
What are you hoping for today?

.... | ....
.... | ....
.... | ....
.... | ....
.... | ....
.... | ....
.... | ....
.... | ....
.... | ....
.... | ....
.... | ....
.... | ....
.... | ....
.... | ....
.... | ....
.... | ....
.... | ....
.... | ....
.... | ....
.... | ....
.... | ....
.... | ....
.... | ....

If You Want, Give

Inspiration
Life is about giving what you want; if you want love, give it. If you want friends, be a friend. Everything you want is in your hand.

Reflection
What do you need to give today?

Inspiration
Tomorrow doesn't belong to you, but today is yours—Will you show up?

Reflection
When was the last time you pressed to show up? What was the outcome?

Life is taking care of one another

Inspiration
Life is not the survival of the fittest; it's about taking care of one another.

Reflection
Who do you know that needs care today?

Lift Others

Inspiration
Elevation comes when we lift others.

Reflection
Commit to market one of your sisters today. Toot their horn.

We ned windows of opportunity

Inspiration
We cannot let fear or the need to ponder make us miss windows of opportunity.

Reflection
What has fear cost you? What will you redeem?

Inspiration

We may not be fine at this moment, but we will be fine.

Reflection

Do you believe that? Why?

Keep looking higher

Inspiration
Whatever the obstacle, keep looking higher.

Reflection
What do you see?

Expect great things

Inspiration
Be an optimist, expect great things.

Reflection
For the next seven days, commit to seeing everything through the lens of an optimist.

....

Inspiration

Whatever the chapter of your life, finish the book.

Reflection

What chapter are you on? How long have you been in that chapter? Is it time to turn the page?

Recognize Purpose

Recognize Purpose

Shani Richards
Purpose Partner

As you journey through these pages, I invite you to move forward with curiosity and commitment. Curiosity to discover or rediscover aspects of you that are easy to overlook and are utterly fantastic.

They are the parts of you that can be undervalued because they come so easy and have been there in some instances since childhood. Commitment to focus on who you really are rather than who you think you are supposed to be. Explore the thoughts and memories that point you toward what you have always wanted and longed to do but have grown content to look upon as a distant memory. Be willing to take those 'shelved' dreams and goals and re-examine them with a curiosity and a commitment to be every bit of who you are fabulously.

Your success isn't out of reach

Recognition

Fulfilling your purpose will only cost you everything that is in your way.
Your success isn't out of reach or over the rainbow, but it is right on the other side of fear, weariness, and possibly preoccupation of what other people think. When we surrender obstacles, we gain the sure footing, confidence, and clarity that we will need to navigate our new success territory.

Reflection

- What are you determined to go for?
- What consistently blocks you?
- What is newly blocking you?
- What moves can you make to climb, go around or power through what's in front of you?

See what you want before it manifests

Recognition

Just because you want what you don't have doesn't mean you want what you can't have. You have to see what you want in your mind's eye and consider it a done deal before you actually see it manifested. So no, you're not mistaken if you're the only one who sees your vision before it manifests. Manufacturers, artists, crafters, inventors, architects – they all see what they are creating before it actually is perfected and presented. That means that when we're working towards our vision, we are in the draft, prototype and testing phases.

Reflection

What are you working towards that you are ready to fully see? Describe or draw it. What phase are you in?

.... | ....
.... | ....
.... | ....
.... | ....
.... | ....
.... | ....
.... | ....
.... | ....
.... | ....
.... | ....
.... | ....
.... | ....
.... | ....
.... | ....
.... | ....
.... | ....
.... | ....
.... | ....
.... | ....
.... | ....
.... | ....
.... | ....
.... | ....

Recognition

We aren't all climbing the same mountains. So, I'll see you at the top of yours as I'm standing at the top of mine! We aren't in competition with each other, we're really our own competition, to do our best each day. That means there's room at the top because what we're trying to accomplish, even if it looks similar, is different.

Reflection

- What actions or people in your area(s) of interest are inspirational?
- What is something that you have done or are doing that others have told you they admire?
- What have you created or contributed to that you sincerely admire (don't be shy)? Even if you are the only one who noticed.
- To be proud of yourself in your current effort/work/project, who do you have to be?

Recognition

You created the life you have. What do you need to create to have the life you want? We can either live by default or by intention. Default living means that whatever has happened will continue to happen, while living with intention creates effort and action that reroutes us to have the outcome that we plan for and focus on.

Reflection

- What aspects of your life do you sense are connected to your purpose and are currently on the 'shelf' rather than actively engaged?
- What are your biggest concerns about getting started right now?
- If what you wanted for your life was guaranteed to happen the moment you said so, what's missing? What needs to be subtracted? When do you want it to happen?

Create the life you'd risk it all to have

Recognition

You've been careful to create the life you have. What is the life you'd risk it all to have?

Reflection

- What in your life have you outgrown?
- What new adventure are you excited, nervous and even doubtful to take on?
- What headline can you create to describe you doing what may be totally unexpected, but sincerely is a vision you have for your life?

Life's seasons change

Recognition

Like the weather, life's seasons change. Are you properly dressed for your season? Sometimes we head into the day or a situation and get seemingly drenched by an onslaught of conditions that we realize we could have been prepared for. Or, perhaps whatever we encountered was a complete surprise. While there is no surefire way to anticipate every situation, condition, or reaction, there is a way that we can prepare for what we know will happen or even for surprises. For instance, walking into an emotional situation can feel like entering into a storm with torrents of complicated emotions, essentially an emotional downpour. Do we get soaked? Do we retreat? Perhaps, or we may choose to understand what we need to carry with us to weather the storms.

Reflection

- What situations seem to defeat you every time or most times?
- What can you do to honor how you want to show up? Before the situation | In the situation | After the situation.

The Vision Partner Journal

Finishing creates confidence

Recognition

Focus so you can finish. Sometimes and in some seasons in our lives, we can be so eager to start, but find ourselves stumped, frustrated or bored by continuing to the finish line. It isn't unusual to start something new while something is in progress. But, it can be a red flag or a concern if you find yourself looking to start something new to distract you from what you haven't finished. Finishing is important because it creates and communicates confidence and reliability internally and externally.

Reflection

- What are the projects or tasks that you started and realize it is important to finish?
- Knowing yourself as you do, what distractions do you eagerly or willingly take on that derails your progress?
- Knowing your day and capacity, what steps towards finishing will you take today?

Reignite your passion

Recognition

Go beyond remembering...reignite your passion to pursue your purpose! Sometimes knowingly or unknowingly we put ideas and intentions on the shelf. We can lose track, especially if our creativity generates ideas on a daily, sometimes hourly basis. In our tendency to be attracted to or create new things to begin, we can sometimes overlook or abandon the seemingly ordinary thing that excites us in pursuit of that next thing. When we continuously pursue what we aren't good at, we can miss noticing what we truly desire to do. Clues to passion and purpose are patterned through our life's seasons. It can oftentimes be unacknowledged by us while being acknowledged or even praised by others.

Reflection

- Today, write down a list of areas, skill sets, and/or abilities that you have had over quite a few years.
- List areas, skill sets, and/or abilities that you have received praise for but were not fully in agreement that it was praiseworthy.
- Can you see anything on your list that you wish that you could do more of and/or more consistently?
- What action can you take today to revisit that area, skill set and/or ability? This could be placing a phone call to speak with an old partner, colleague, etc. This could also look like turning on the music and revisiting a familiar dance routine or just freestyling it.

Your thoughts are your truth

Recognition

No matter what anyone thinks or says about you, whatever you think or say about you is right. Essentially, your thoughts are your truth and every thought that someone expresses about you has to pass through the checkpoint of your thoughts. Your thoughts will magnetically invite all positive or negative thoughts that align with and support them. The beauty is that it may take weeks, months or years for someone to change their mind about you. It may take a long time for others to change what they say about you, but the instant that you choose to think differently, the moment your thought changes, you are right.

Reflection

- You are writing on the pages of your story, day by day and decision by decision.
- What decision is it important for you to make that changes your story in a desired way?
- Write a desired part of your story that you will focus on today.
- For instance if your story used to be (even up until a moment ago) that you eat beyond fullness to manage stress, you can write your story to say that you eat until you are satisfied and that you manage your emotions and stress through moving your body, meditation, prayer, stillness, acceptance, etc.
- Make edits to your story in bits and in ways that are manageable for you to complete swiftly and confidently.
- Commit your focus and energy to live out and express what you have written.

Recognition

Right now, every day, you are practicing who you are and who you will be.

Reflection

- List 5 things that you currently do that you know contributes to your goals. This represents who you are proud to be and want to remain.
- List 5 things that you currently do that you suspect or know hinders you from reaching your goals: This represents opportunities to grow beyond your obstacles and distractions.
- List 5 things that you used to do that you no longer do that you now understand would be beneficial to you reaching your goals: This represents your ability to overcome challenges and to have forward focus.
- List 5 things that you no longer do that you used to do, and you recognize that it was hindering you: This represents your ability and practice of moving forward in freedom.

The *Vision Partner* **Journal**

www.ingramcontent.com/pod-product-compliance
Lightning Source LLC
Chambersburg PA
CBHW050804220426
43209CB00089BA/1690